Charlie Wright

Would You Rather... Game Book

For Kids 6-12 Years Old

© 2019 by Charlie Wright

Printed in the United States of America

How to Play.

The rules are very basic.
To start the game:

- You need at least two players.

- Choose the first one.
He or she will choose the
question for the next player.

- All questions begin with
the phrase "Would you rather…?"
and ends with two possible
funny or thought-provoking
scenarios to choose from.

•Next person should pick an answer from two given scenarios.

The main thing is to pick something.

One can't answer "both" or "none".

•You can play until you have creative ideas or until someone won't be able to make a choice.

The only rule that cannot be broken is that of having fun! Have a nice game!

Would You Rather...

Be a turtle
or
a rabbit?

Would You Rather...

Would You Rather...

Eat chocolate cake
or
pumpkin pie?

Would You Rather...

Spend time with
your grandparents
or
friends?

Would You Rather...

Eat sweets
or
fruits?

'Would You Rather...

Be a wizard
or
a superhero?

Would You Rather...

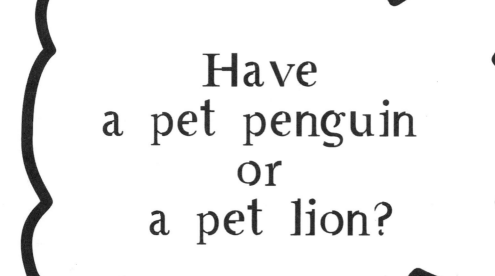

Have
a pet penguin
or
a pet lion?

Would You Rather...

Dance
or
sing?

Would You Rather...

Be a unicorn
or
a dinosaur?

Would You Rather...

Be able to create
a new holiday
or
create a new
game?

Eat a worm
or
a grasshopper?

Would You Rather...

Ask silly questions
or
answer them?

Have a
purple nose
or
green ears?

Would You Rather...

Be able to fly
like a bird
or
swim like a fish?

Have 4 legs
or
5 arms?

Would You Rather...

Become five
years older
or
two years
younger?

Play soccer
or
baseball?

Would You Rather...

Be friends with
superman
or
spiderman?

Go to the doctor
or
to the dentist?

Would You Rather...

Use a bag
or
a backpack?

Be able to
control fire
or
water?

Would You Rather...

Brush your teeth
with soap
or
drink sour juice?

Eat donuts
or
candy?

Would You Rather...

Have 9 brothers
or
8 sisters?

Be able to talk
to dogs
or
cats?

Would You Rather...

Eat a whole
raw onion
or
a whole lemon?

Have
super strength
or
super speed?

Would You Rather...

Kiss a frog
or
hug a lizard?

Have a twin
or
be the only child?

Would You Rather...

Visit somebody
or
have a
guest at home?

Drink
orange juice
or
milk?

Would You Rather...

Take a shower
or
have a bath?

Fly an airplane
or
drive a
fire truck?

Would You Rather...

Play outdoors
or
indoors?

Kiss a jellyfish
or
step on
a hedgehog?

Would You Rather...

Lose your
sense of taste
or
your sense
of smell?

Become
someone else
or
just stay you?

Would You Rather...

Play with
the snow
or
play with
the sand?

Eat-in bed
or
in the bathroom?

Would You Rather...

Eat cat food
or
dog food?

Always be tired
or
always be hungry?

Would You Rather...

Live forever
or
be given unlimited candy?

Watch movies
or
cartoons?

Would You Rather...

Be one of
Santa's elves
or
be one of Santa's
reindeer?

Visit the circus
or
the zoo?

Would You Rather...

Be invisible
or
be able to fly?

Get up
very early
or
stay up
very late?

Would You Rather...

Jump into a pool
or
into a pile
of leaves?

Catch a big fish
or
many little fish?

Would You Rather...

Be like
an Iron Man
or
a Halk for a day?

Give a high-five
or
handshake?

Would You Rather...

Get a cake baked
by a 6-year-old baker
or
get a haircut from a
12-year-old hairdresser?

Feel sleepy
during the day
or
always have
insomnia at night?

Would You Rather...

Read Diary of a
Wimpy kid
or
Diary of
Minecraft Zombie?

Watch a boring
adult movie
or
a baby movie?

Would You Rather...

Eat 10 tacos
or
10 pizzas?

Live in Narnia
or go
to school
at Hogwarts?

Would You Rather...

Be very short
or
extremely tall?

Live in a place
that is always dusty
or
always humid?

Would You Rather...

Not be able
to sit
or
not be able
to stand?

Live out in
the country
or
in the city?

Would You Rather...

Be a giant mouse
or
a tiny elephant?

Have a submarine
or
a space shuttle?

Would You Rather...

Not be able
to read
or
not be able
to write?

Be a boss
or
an employee?

Would You Rather...

Be always overdressed
or
underdressed?

Be SpongeBob
or
be Patrick?

Would You Rather...

Get 10$
today
or
get 1$ a day for
20 days?

Only drink
Coca cola
or
only drink
Pepsi?

Would You Rather...

Explore space
or
find a new ocean?

Have
x-ray vision
or
magnified
hearing?

Would You Rather...

Have many
good friends
or
one very
best friend?

Be stuck
on a train
or
a bus?

Would You Rather...

Change your
eye color
or
your hair color?

Eat no candy
at Halloween
or
no turkey
at Thanksgiving?

Would You Rather...

Speak all
languages
or
be able to speak
to all animals?

Have a foot
long nose
or
a foot
long tongue?

Would You Rather...

Look like a fish
or
smell like a fish?

Be a silly teacher
or
an evil doctor?

Would You Rather...

Be without
elbows
or
be without knees?

Have a dragon
or
be a dragon?

Would You Rather...

Live forever
or
eat unlimited
candy?

Only be able
to whisper
or
only be able to
shout everything?

Would You Rather...

Fart every
time you laugh
or
every time
you cry?

Never play
or
play but
always lose?

Would You Rather...

Be toilet paper
or
cut paper?

Live without
music
or
live without tv?

Would You Rather...

Be a kid
your whole life
or
an adult your
whole life?

Have unlimited
games
or
have unlimited
snacks?

Would You Rather...

Be a cow
or
a chicken?

Be the smartest
kid in school
or
the most popular?

Would You Rather...

Watch TV
all day
or
meet someone
new each day?

Learn to swim
fast
or
learn to dive
for longer?

Would You Rather...

Have a
horse's tail
or
a unicorn horn?

Be in your
pajamas
or
a suit all day?

Would You Rather...

Eat a spoon
of wasabi
or
a spoon of salt?

Swim in a pool
full of zombie
or
full of sharks?

Would You Rather...

Take an
art class
or
take a
music class?

Watch a comedy
or
a scary movie?

Would You Rather...

Be able to travel into the future
or
into the past?

Lose your memory
or
lose your best friend?

Would You Rather...

Eat spaghetti
with a spoon
or
eat pizza with
chopsticks?

Get stung
by a bee
or
eat a poisonous
mushroom?

Would You Rather...

Fall from a ship
or
fall from a
roller coaster
and stay alive?

Eat one raw egg
or
ten cooked eggs?

Would You Rather...

Have a nose
of a dog
or
eyes of a cat?

Be popular with
fake friends
or
be losers with
a true friend?

Would You Rather...

Go to school
365 days a year
or
never get
an education?

Eat a live snail
or
eat a dead bug?

Would You Rather...

Have to wear
1 color each day
or
wear all 7 colors
every day?

Live somewhere
that is always hot
or
always cold?

Would You Rather...

Control
the future
or
control
the weather?

Have five hours of
homework a day
or
never have
summer break?

Would You Rather...

Wake up in a
deep forest
or
wake up in a
desert?

Sell freshly
squeezed lemonade
or
try to find a new
home for 10 kittens?

Would You Rather...

Go to
summer school
or
math camp?

Watch a
football game
or
a basketball
game?

Would You Rather...

Travel by road
or
by air?

Surf the internet
or
surf the ocean?

Would You Rather...

Learn how
to cook soup
or
learn how
to bake a cake?

Dress fashionably
or
comfortably?

Would You Rather...

Have really
large feet
or
really large
hands?

Prank your parents
or
have your parents
try to prank you?

Would You Rather...

Be a terrible
dancer
or
be a terrible
singer?

Fart loudly in
class
or
in the hallway?

Would You Rather...

Fall off a bike
or
fall off
a skateboard?

Be abducted
by Zombies
or
Aliens?

Would You Rather...

Sneeze really
loud
or
sneeze really
hard?

Be in a
Disney animation
or
in a Disney
movie?

Would You Rather...

Go for a walk
or
drive around
with dad
in his car?

Get a toy boat
or
see a
real-life ship?

Would You Rather...

Listen to
an audiobook
or
read a
hardcover book?

Shower with
cold water
or
hot water?

Would You Rather...

Get a trick
or
a treat?

Go to a
new school
or
move to a
new house?

Would You Rather...

Play games
on a phone
or
play a board
game?

Live in a
tree house
or
on a houseboat?

Would You Rather...

Eat
homemade food
or
fast food?

Sleep in
your bed
or
sleep with
your parents?

Would You Rather...

Parody
Britney Spears
or
Lil Wayne?

Be bald
or
have long hair?

Would You Rather...

Drop with
the rain
or
fall with
the snow?

Use glasses
or
get contact lenses?

Would You Rather...

Sit in the
front
or
in the back
of a school bus?

Face your fears
or
forget you
have fears?

Would You Rather...

Be able to spit
out ice
or
spit out a fire?

Have your
grandmother's
hairstyle
or
her first name?

Would You Rather...

Be able to eat
very fast
or
be able to drink
really fast?

Swim 10 meters
through
the chocolate
or
milkshake pool?

Would You Rather...

Would You Rather...

Reviews

Your reviews are very important! If you have enjoyed this book, please consider leaving a short review on Amazon.

Thank you so much.

Would You Rather... Game Book